DISCOVER PHYSICAL SCIENCE

DISCOVER MAGNETS

Tammy Enz

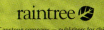
raintree

a Capstone company — publishers for children

Raintree is an imprint of Capstone Global Library Limited, a company incorporated in England and Wales having its registered office at 264 Banbury Road, Oxford, OX2 7DY – Registered company number: 6695582

www.raintree.co.uk
myorders@raintree.co.uk

Edited by Aaron Sautter
Designed by Hilary Wacholz
Original illustrations © Capstone Global Library Limited 2021
Picture research by Jo Miller
Production by Spencer Rosio
Set Styling by Marcy Morin
Originated by Capstone Global Library Ltd
Printed and bound in India

978 1 3982 0225 2 (hardback)
978 1 3982 0226 9 (paperback)

British Library Cataloguing in Publication Data
A full catalogue record for this book is available from the British Library.

Acknowledgements
We would like to thank the following for permission to reproduce photographs: Capstone Studio: Karon Dubke, 5, 11, 21; Shutterstock: Aleksandr Pobedimskiy, 8, Craig Walton, 12, Garsya, 19, haryigit, 15, KRPD, 9, Petar An, Cover, ShutterStockStudio, 7, tkyszk, 13, Tyler Olson, 17. Design Elements: Capstone; Shutterstock: Immersion Imagery.

Every effort has been made to contact copyright holders of material reproduced in this book. Any omissions will be rectified in subsequent printings if notice is given to the publisher.

Contents

Words in **bold** are in the glossary.

MAGICAL MAGNETS

Have you ever played with **magnets**? They can be fun. They stick to each other. They can hold notes on a fridge.

Magnets sometimes seem like magic. They can pick up a whole string of paper clips. Magnets have many uses. But what makes them work?

Magnets have a **force** that can push or pull things. They can move things without touching them. People cannot see this force.

But magnets do not work an all things. They do not stick to plastic, glass or paper. They only stick to some kinds of metal.

HOW MAGNETS ARE MADE

Some magnets are found in **nature**. Some kinds of rock and metal are **magnetic**. They push and pull things just like magnets.

magnetic rock

Most magnets are made by people.
They come in many shapes. Some are
round or shaped like a bar. Some are
shaped like horseshoes.

HOW MAGNETS WORK

Magnets have two **poles**. One is the north pole. The other is the south pole. The poles look the same. But they do not work the same.

Get two magnets. Hold the north and south poles together. What happens? They pull together and stick. It is hard to pull them apart.

Hold the north poles of two magnets together. What happens? The poles push each other away. They don't stick. The two south poles also push each other away.

Hold a north pole near something made of metal. What happens? It pulls towards the metal. It sticks. The south pole sticks to metal too. Both poles pull and **attract** metal.

ELECTRICITY AND MAGNETS

Some magnets are made with **electricity**. When power flows through metal it makes a magnet.

These magnets can be very strong. But they are not like other magnets. They only work until the power stops. They can be turned on and off.

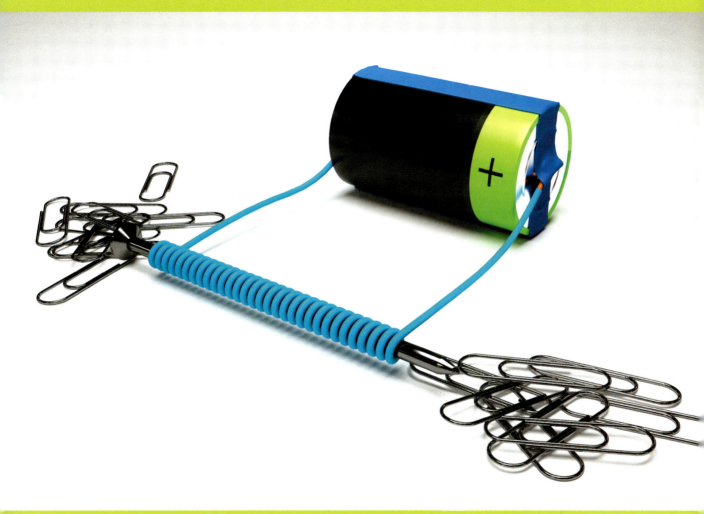

MAGNETS IN OUR WORLD

Magnets have many uses. They are found in many machines. They are used in radio and TV **speakers**. Some big magnets help to lift heavy metal objects.

Doctors use machines with strong magnets. The machines help doctors to see what is inside people's bodies.

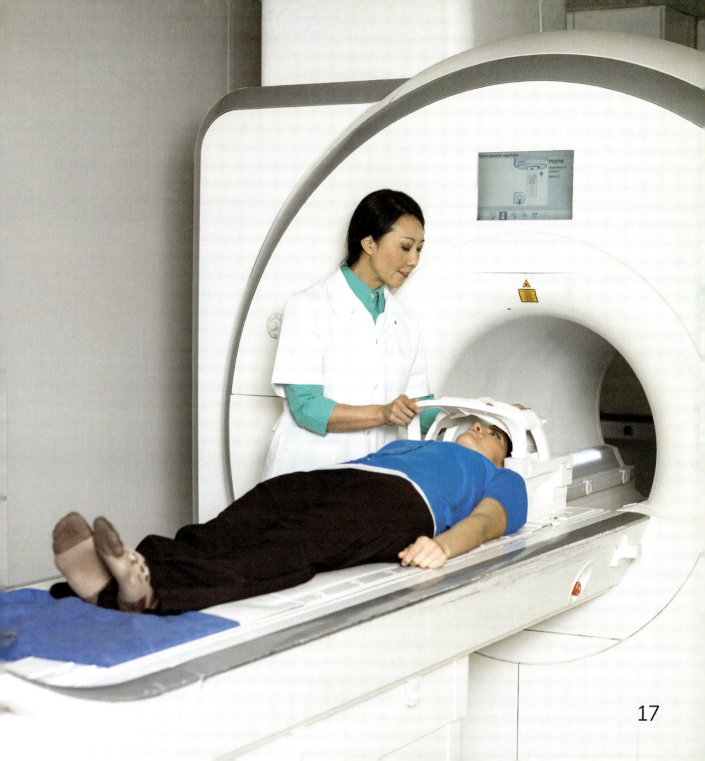

EARTH IS A MAGNET

We live on a giant magnet! The centre of Earth is filled with metal. This metal acts like a magnet. It creates a magnetic field and poles on Earth.

Compasses use magnets. They point at Earth's poles. They help people find their way. Magnets are useful. They are found in things we use every day.

compass

MAKE A MAGNET WAND

Supplies:

2 small round fridge magnets

1 wooden craft stick

glue

1 plastic button

1 metal paper clip

5 x 5-centimetre (2 x 2-inch) piece of paper

5 x 5-centimetre (2 x 2-inch) piece of tin foil

5-cm (2-inch) piece of pipe cleaner

Directions:

1. Glue one magnet to the end of the craft stick.

2. Lay out the other objects.

3. Test each item with the wand. Which items stick to the magnet wand? Keep track of which items stick. Why do you think they stick?

Glossary

attract pull and hold

compass tool that points to Earth's poles

electricity flowing energy

force something that pushes or pulls

magnet something that attracts metal; magnets have a north and a south pole

magnetic able to act like a magnet

nature everything in the natural world that is not made by people

pole end of a magnet

speaker part of a radio, TV or other device that creates sound

Find out more

Books

Experiments with Magnets (Read and Experiment), Isabel Thomas (Raintree, 2016)

Forces and Magnets (Moving up with Science), Peter Riley (Franklin Watts, 2016)

What is Magnetism? (Science Basics), Mark Weakland (Raintree, 2019)

Websites

www.bbc.co.uk/bitesize/clips/zhvfb9q
Watch this BBC Bitesize video about powerful magnets.

www.dkfindout.com/uk/science/forces-and-motion/gravity/
Find out more about gravity with DKfindout!

Index